Introduction

I was born in West London 56 years ago and getting interested in nature was never a problem.

There were fewer cars, less major roads, ample parks and lots of little corners of waste land where nature could thrive. But London started to spread its wings into neighbouring counties and with it brought more cars, major roads, motorways and housing developments.

All the little corners have now gone mostly to property developers. Wildlife struggles on the best it can but in most cases it seems to be fighting a losing battle.

I moved to the borders of Surrey twenty-six years ago to the small village of Shepperton, where between work I have explored new areas of wildlife and habitats.

As a young lad I had the usual collection of birds eggs and while collecting them I got hooked on birdwatching. I have read old books on London when otters were frequently seen as near to London as Kew Bridge on the river Thames. This I have never seen, but Red Backed Shrikes on Hounslow Heath, I have, along with many other species that have been forced out or disappeared all together.

After moving to Shepperton, I became even more interested in bird watching and began to study it in more detail. It was while walking around the Queen Mary Reservoir that I met Ron Wells, a local bird photographer who introduced me to bird photography.

I purchased by first camera, a second-hand Zenith and a cheap 125mm lens. But when the shutter clicked it went off like a gun, hence I started to compile a collection of blurred bird photographs. This was all part of learning bird photography Ron told me.

I continued to persue my new hobby quite happily and even started to give a few talks and slide shows of my efforts to local clubs and guilds. Gradually wild areas were disappearing all around me.

Fields one day – houses the next;
Fields one day – roads the next;
Streams re-routed
The River Thames choked-up with boats and people
persuing their own hobbies.

So I started to move further afield to persue mine. That's how I met Cliff who became a close friend and this book was eventually put together about bird life with factual stories. Hence the title *Seeing is Believing*.

Cliff has helped me tremendously with the photographic side of my birdwatching and together we have enjoyed many ventures. Another friend of mine, Bill Lowe also shared some of these early days which will be explained on another page.

When Cliff or myself are photographing, the welfare of the birds is more important than the photographs. A licence is needed to photograph some specific birds, but certain precautions are always taken, such as never putting up a hide where it may attract other people's attention. So most of the photography is carried out on private land with the owner's permission.

To sit in a hide is most rewarding as you soon discover that like most humans, birds are individuals. Some birds are very wary so the utmost care is taken to ensure their safety and sometimes it's best to leave the birds alone.

Some birds seem to be oblivious to a hide or camera and it's these that have produced some of the most enjoyable memories.

Cliff lives in the small village of Abinger, so between us we try to cover as many areas as we can. Usually we both finish up in our favourite spots to study fewer birds but in more detail.

As I have already mentioned, some areas have now gone, so we try and capture our photographs where we can, and I try to record all the stories. I am not so much a photographer but someone who birdwatches through the lens of a camera.

This book contains just some of the many photographs, stories, poems and experiences compiled while persuing my favourite hobby.

Two Men and Their Dogs

Bill Lowe has to have a special mention in my book because it was with him and his dogs that we learnt so much together about our local wildlife. Bill before he went to work used to come out to Shepperton most mornings to collect weeds and seeds for his aviary birds.

We became good friends and together with our dogs spent many happy hours persuing our hobby.

Most of the time it seemed that we were saving ground nesting birds from the crows, magpies and motor bikes. Yes motor bikes! For in those early days there was more gravel being extracted and the land used to be left barren for ages. This became good habitat for such birds as the Little Ringed Plovers, Ringed Plovers, Lapwings, Skylarks, Redshanks and Meadow Pippits.

But the motor bike riders were unaware of the birds and Bill and myself had several confrontations with them. This was to no avail, so we tried to educate the bikers by actually showing them where the nests were located. We showed them eggs and young birds that they could possibly run over.

From that day they changed their attitude and pursued their hobby well away from the nesting birds.

Bill and another birdwatcher, Richard Holliman were also responsible for building the terns raft on one of the gravel pits which is explained in one of my stories.

I have a lot of memories from those early days with Bill and the dogs. Most of them Bill captured on ciné film and I with my old Zenith camera. Some of the audiences we gave our talks to unfortunately had to share them.

We were a good team and between us we helped to save many a nesting bird, and that's a memory worth keeping.

◀ Bill deep in concentration.
❖ Camera crew at the ready.

Seeing is Believing

by
Derek Belsey

One day while photographing a Robin on a local allotment, the bird found my tripod an ideal perch to watch out for worms being turned over in the soil. So I took this shot with my other camera.

This is just one of the many things to happen during bird watching as many of my stories will explain.

Contents

All photographs by the author
with the exception of some by
Clifford Reddick

ISBN 0 9530734 0 8
© Derek Belsey 1997

Published by Derek Belsey
Tel: 01932 241886

Designed by Abbey Graphics,
Printed by Ian Allan Printing Ltd.

Snap Happy Blackbirds

Our resident Blackbirds chose a conifer in the front garden this Spring for their home. I watched her from my lounge window building their nest with her mate always in close attendance. She laid a clutch of four eggs of which three hatched.

After a few days had passed, I thought I would try to get a photograph. There was no chance of using my hide, so I set the camera up on a tripod with a cable release, with the lens focused up on the nest. I retired to a safe distance behind another conifer. Remembering how shy the last pair of Blackbirds were that I photographed, I did not feel too confident of getting a picture.

◀ Snap-happy Blackbird.　　　　▲ 'Me camera shy?' Never!

To my surprise, it was not long before the hen bird showed herself on the front gate with a large beak full of worms. Then she flew straight to the conifer. I waited a few seconds then pressed the cable release hoping for some sort of a picture.

After quite some while, she had not flown out of the conifer. I slowly and quietly tip-toed towards the camera and looking through the lens could hardly believe my eyes. There she sat brooding her young, oblivious of my presence. So I slowly focussed up again and pressed the shutter, not a movement from the caring mother. I took some more beautiful pictures while the mother and young continually posed for the camera.

I returned to the house because while all this was going on the cock bird had not once returned to the nest. I was no sooner back inside and looking out through the window when there he was sitting on the wall with a beak full of goodies for the young.

I suppose he had now taken over the nest, preening his feathers for the next photo session, who knows?

A Robin's Retreat

Almost everybody loves to see a Robin in their garden as they seem to be the boldest of our smaller birds. They will defend their territory at all costs and at times become quite fierce. Robins will also nest in the most peculiar places.

It's not a matter of where I've found them nesting but where they have not. I could name many but here I just mention a few that I've found.

One pair nested in a crane that was extracting gravel from one of my local pits. Both birds followed the crane up and down the pit all day long to feed their young. Anther pair nested in a washing peg bag in the garden of a friend. The cock Robin would attack anyone that approached the peg bag. It resulted in many trips down to the local launderette until the Robins had flown away.

One Robin even nested in another friend's hanging flower basket as late as September. Only the female brooded and then raised a brood with a little help of a daily supply of mealworms.

I have hidden in my garden all types of bird boxes, cans, kettles and an old tea pot.

My pair of Robins have nested in most of them but their last effort was in my tool shed tucked away behind some tins of wood dye.

A pair of Cliff's Robins seemed to have a sweet tooth because they nested in a Cadburys Chocolate Box.

The list is endless but I need the next page for another bird story.

◀ A Robin named 'Peggy'.
❧ This bird hitches a free ride on a crane.

MY ROBIN

He perches high for all to see
My Robin in his territory
No other Redbreast dares to enter
In my Robin's Garden Centre
If he does it won't be long
Before he hears the battle gong
The fight takes place and feathers fly
But it's over soon and I know why
My Robin stays here all year round
And as of yet, yields no ground
When he's won you can hear him sigh
With chest puffed out and head held high
He calls his mate "I've won again"
As he flies about in their safe domain.

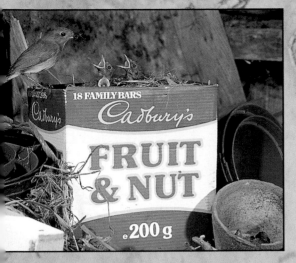

▲ A real fruit and nut case.
Dye-ing to feed its young. ▼

▲This bird I called the flower girl.

Seeing Jays, the Hard Way

One of our most colourful birds but, in my opinion, one of the most roguish is the Jay, who will take eggs and young of most other birds. I've witnessed this on many occasions.

One of these times was when I was photographing a Moorhen, about to hatch out her young. On leaving the nest the first young Moorhen was taken by a pike. Of course this alarmed both parent birds and they fled, but it was not long before the female returned to the comfort of her nest to continue her hatching programme. Whilst watching this scene I heard what I thought was a songbird. I was amazed when I looked through the side of my hide where I had the camera hidden to see that it was in fact, a Jay. It was making the most beautiful soft song and it was almost hypnotising a young Moorhen and the pair of adults who were calling to their youngster from a short distance away. Gradually the Jay got closer to the nest, ready to take the young Moorhen. It was now time for me to intervene. I clapped my hands and the Jay flew off. But I knew that it was only a matter of time before it returned to take the chick and the remaining eggs. Indeed, I've actually seen a Jay snatch young Moorhens and Coots off the water like a bird of prey.

My friend, Ron, found a Jay's nest on Ashford Manor Golf Course. To photograph it, he made up a hide from a pair of high footsteps with a platform nailed to one of the rungs. This contraption we put in place, well camouflaged ready for getting the young Jays on film when they hatched. I was the first to attempt the necessary contortion as I will now explain: I had to sit on the top rung with the hide erected over me. It wasn't long before my legs started to ache and become numb. To say it was uncomfortable would be an understatement. Fortunately, the parent birds returned to the nest and I took some very pleasing pictures.

I learnt several things on this caper. One of them was that Jays regurgitate their food. Another was that feeding times were few and far between. Two and a half hours, to be precise.

▲ Jays at their best.　　　▼ A Jay at his worst.

A Pair of Persevering Long Tailed Tits

I had been watching a pair of Long Tailed Tits building their nest over a period of almost a week. The nest unfortunately was in quite an open position in some brambles and I feared Magpies would find it.

My fears were proved right for on my next visit I startled a pair of Magpies that were pulling the nest to bits. I knew by now the Tits must have eggs and the chances of them being in tact were slim. I felt into the nest and could just make out some eggs, so I patched up the nest as best I could before retiring to a safe distance to watch for either the Magpies or Tits to return.

To my surprise the Magpies did not return, but above me in the tree tops I could hear the Tits which gave me some hope. I collected some old bits of bramble and tried to make the nest more secure and hopefully deter the Magpies.

I went back home to collect some chicken wire to put over and around the nest. This having been successful in the past. On arriving back it was obvious that the Magpies had attacked the nest again. I still put up the chicken wire and left the scene with little confidence.

Three days passed and I returned to find no sign of the Tits and their nest was still in a sorry state. I felt into the nest once more, there were still eggs but they were stone cold. I left feeling rather despondent but as I normally do I was back in the area a few days later and naturally I had to have a look at the bedraggled nest. But a nice surprise awaited me, the nest had been tidied up and a few minor repairs had been made. I looked a bit closer, and I could just make out a little face of a Long Tailed Tit.

I again retired to a safe distance to watch for her mate to return. It was not long before he did, with more nesting material for maintenance purposes. The happy outcome two weeks later was the five young Long Tailed Tits being fed in their patched up home by their persevering parents.

As I walked home I thought of that well-known saying – "If at first you don't succeed try, try and try again".

A lesson for us all. ❡ The nest that's a work of art.

> ## LONG TAILED TIT
>
> *A Long Tailed Tits nest is a work of art*
> *And it's built with painstaking care*
> *The Birds both flit and dart*
> *To build the nest with moss and hair*
> *Litchen and cobwebs are also used*
> *As both birds work together*
> *Materials then are carefully fused*
> *And then filled with the occasional feather*
> *An occasional feather? I try to deceive*
> *2,000 when finished I'm led to believe.*

The Farm

Both farming and gravel extraction methods are commonly criticised by naturalists, ornithologists and national newspapers. The picture they paint is of sterile fields deserted by wildlife. But in truth is frequently quite different.

On Charles Bransden's 95ha (230-acre) intensive vegetable farm at Laleham near Chertsey, Surrey, both farming and gravel extraction go hand in hand with concern for nature and wildlife.

The farm – which specialises in growing relatively exotic vegetables like coriander, kohlrabi, chinese cabbage and fennel – is not in an idyllic out-of-the-way setting either. It is close to the M3, and Heathrow Airport is just seven miles away.

Gravel has been extracted for many years by the farm's owners, Greenham Construction Materials. Once the gravel has been removed the soil is put back again and farming resumes. While all this is happening I keep an eye out for the birds and have noticed that many nesting birds are flourishing.

After one particular period of extraction the farm's owners created a small lake with landscaping, trees and shrubs established around it. The lake is now mature and supports a resident pair of Little Grebes that have nested successfully for the past two years. Coots, Mallards, Moorhens, Tufted Ducks and a pair of Swans also frequent the lake.

All this despite the fact that vegetable production involves some of the most intensive farming methods used in Britain. There are many passes with tractors as well as with irrigation rigs.

Sprayer operator Garry Nicholls keeps alert for nesting birds on the ground he is covering. When he spots one he marks the nest with a stake. The crop pickers are then made aware of this and try to avoid disturbing the nesting birds.

This bird-conscious approach to intensive farming means that Laleham Farm is probably one of the few places locally where you can still see and hear the Skylark as is soars skywards.

◁ A Yellow Wagtail surveys its summer home.

Each year Yellow Wagtails arrive from their wintering grounds abroad to start their courtship displays. I have spent many hours sitting in the fields of onion and kohlrabi fascinated by their behaviour and wondering why they return to this part of the country.

Both Charles Bransden and Garry Nicholls are aware of the benefits to be gained from a little care and consideration, and Skylarks, Yellow Wagtails, Pied Wagtails, Meadow Pipits, Little Ringed Plovers and Lapwings have a high success rate on the farm.

The farm has also planted hedgerows on the restored land and these are host to Goldfinches, Greenfinches, Linnets and Dunnocks. The gravel pit attracts Kingfishers, Coots, Moorhens, Common Terns and Great Crested Grebes.

One thing that cannot be avoided is giving nesting birds an occasional dousing with water from the irrigators. But the birds seem to survive. In fact it is not the farming methods that destroy nests on this farm but the resident Crows that work the fields and take ground-nesting fledglings.

These and other distractions have prompted some of the birds to nest in peculiar places. A Robin in a crane, a Pied Wagtail in an excavator, a Skylark on the side of the road. A little Ringed Plover has even nested in the middle of a road and a Yellow Wagtail will nest in any crop you care to mention.

In the winter wildlife still flourishes, with flocks of Geese working the fields over, feeding on the stubble and odd root vegetables they find.

Snipe and Wheatears are also evident, while back on the gravel pit, Herons, Cormorants, Gulls, Golden Eyes, Shelducks, Shovellers and many other water fowl drop in for a feed.

Nor is the local human population unaware of the wildlife haven that the farm has become. Charles Bransden encourages school parties to tour the farm on educational trips. He supervises them himself and doesn't charge, believing that the educational benefits are reward enough.

The Authers second home around Springtime. ❡

⬥ The Lapwing returns.

⬥ The Ringed Plover is still a farm visitor.
Goldfinch in the morning sun. ❡

Meddling with a Mallard

◀ One very obstinate Duck.

our local working man's club he would be out shooting or ferreting for rabbits.

He was also a very good story-teller, so one night while we were having a drink together and he was telling me about the duck. I had to try and work out whether he was telling the truth or was it another yarn.

Jim asked me if I thought a Mallard could be lifted off her clutch of eggs. Of course a friendly argument followed with Jim assuring me that he had lifted a duck up off her eggs that day.

He had to move some old gravel working machinery that had been lying idle in the field for months. In doing so he noticed a pair of eyes watching him from the long grass, a Mallard sitting on eggs. Above her head was a considerable amount of heavy machinery. If it were to fall it could result in one dead duck and a large portion of scrambled eggs. The duck sat tight and no matter what Jim did she would not budge an inch. He even tried to prise her off the nest with a piece of wood, but to no avail.

So he thought he would try the impossible and to his amazement, succeeded. He actually picked her up off her eggs while his workmate covered them up and moved the machinery.

Jim then placed the pecking duck back on her nest where she proceeded to turn the eggs and snuggle down again.

This I had to see for myself and a little side bet for a pint of beer was wagered. After visiting the nest and finding a successful brood being hatched out and the mother unperturbed by my close presence. I realised that Jim's story had been fact and not one of his countryman's yarns.

Next time we met in the club Jim enjoyed yet another free pint as we talked about this amazing duck.

The Mallard is known to nest in some peculiar places and if disturbed sometimes will fly off and desert her eggs.

This particular duck was different in many ways. As this short story will explain.

An old friend of mine Jim, who unfortunately died a few years ago told me about this unusual bird. Jim was a real outdoors man who worked for one of our local gravel firms. More often than not if he was not having a drink or two in

△ One very caring Duck.

Heron-Call at Kempton Park

The Heronry at Kempton Park was today's choice of venue. I was looking forward to an interesting, if non-eventful day.

But on arriving I spotted some lads chasing what appeared to be an injured Heron. As I approached they ran off, leaving a rather bedraggled young bird flapping along the racecourse. I went back to the car and collected an old coat. I managed to corner the bird then threw the coat over it and took a firm hold on it. Surprisingly, it immediately settled down in my arms without a struggle – obviously, a very frightened and exhausted young Heron.

Now I had rescued the bird, but where should I put it? I tried to place it beneath the Heronry, but noticed that there were still a lot of youngsters about and I realised that it's chances of being left unharassed were slim. So I decided to take the bird home with me and phone Inspector Danby, our local RSPCA man.

I arrived home quite quickly and put the Heron in our back garden, where it just stood motionless.

After a telephone conversation with the RSPCA we agreed that the safest place for the bird was back in the Heronry in an area frequented by most of the adult birds. This, I volunteered to do as I knew the area well and it would save the Inspector a journey from Kingston upon Thames.

As I put the phone down I heard shouting, coming from the back garden. I dashed out to find my son, Neil, trying to prevent the Heron from getting to our small pond. He was unsuccessful, and the hungry Heron sprang to life and sorted out for himself my largest goldfish. I was just in time to see it disappearing down his long neck.

Next, my old cat appeared, drawn by curiosity about this intruder. Quick as lightning, the Heron thrust its large beak at the cat's head and, fortunately, missed it by a fraction of an inch. He was lucky to get away with both eyes in tact. The last I saw of the cat was a pair of very scared eyes, peering out from beneath one of the conifers in the garden.

It was time for the Heron to go. I grabbed it and off we went to Kempton Park. I placed it in the middle of the racecourse by the edge of the gravel pit where most of the Herons fish at regular intervals.

I returned to my car and watched from a distance. It wasn't long before some other Herons flew down and joined it. The young Heron had obviously learned how to feed. I was pleased to see that the bird's day ended better than it had started. By the time I left for home it had eaten several frogs. Not to mention my goldfish.

⊿ Heron at sunset.

THE HERON

Eyes of steel and beak of the same
Stalking a fish his only aim
Standing erect with head very still
Patiently waiting to make just one kill
His thrust must be sure, true and correct
Or it's back to the position of standing erect.

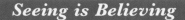
The Brave Little Ringed Plover

This bird, I'm sure, has nerves of steel. I've studied it for years and it never ceases to amaze me – as the following two stories illustrate. The bird's antics have given me many amusing hours. It is amusing, but braver than it is sensible.

It was Jim who showed me the first pair of Plovers locally, on the gravel pit where he worked. I watched them for quite some time, the cock bird making himself easy to see while the female made towards her clutch of four eggs in a zig-zag manner.

I found the nest with the eggs amazingly-camouflaged in the shingle, and on returning a few days later found that one chick had started to peck through its shell. I watched from a safe distance. After about fifteen minutes the brooding bird left the nest with an empty eggshell in her beak, which she deposited at least twenty yards away. She returned to continue her incubating and had just settled down when a cock Pheasant passed, not more than ten feet away from her.

The Plover sat motionless, which was just as well, as following the pheasant was a very furtive-looking dog fox, obviously looking for a meal for its cubs which were occupying an earth that I knew of. The second chick hatched out and Mother again deposited the eggshell at a safe distance from the nest. Next on the scene was a Crow, who flew down and landed not too far from the two chicks and eggs. From nowhere, the cock Plover returned and with its mate saw off the Crow.

After these alarms the rest of the hatching went smoothly and once all the chicks were dry they left the nest and both parents began the task of feeding them. Although I knew they were there, the chicks were so well camouflaged it was almost impossible to pick them out from

▲ Sitting bird ever aware of passing traffic.

the shingle and pebbles.

I returned from time to time to watch again until the chicks grew up.

I have found that the Little Ringed Plover seems almost to invite danger, just as the pair in the first story did by making their nest in the middle of a shingle road that lorries used throughout the day.

The following year the birds returned to find that the landscape had altered as more gravel had been shifted. There were many more lorries driving criss-cross over the remaining gravel but the Plovers decided they could rear another family in this place. After spotting one of the birds running away from the side of a moving lorry I walked up the roadway to find four eggs no more than four feet from the well-worn tyre tracks. I called the site foreman over and explained about the nest. All the drivers came and looked at the eggs. A metal marker was placed on the side of the nest and the drivers used this to keep clear. Thanks to care and patience it worked and four chicks were again safely reared.

Each year they return and each time they nest in some precarious position yet, to the best of my knowledge, they always win.

THE LITTLE RINGED PLOVER

A scrape in the ground without any cover
Is the nesting site of the little ringed plover
She'll sit very tight when danger's around
While he'll show himself high on the ground.
Then lead you away from his sitting mate
While she slips off slowly but only to wait
For the danger to go and feeling at rest
Will quickly return to her eggs in the nest.
When their chicks all hatch out they leave the scrape
To become pebbles or stones and to safety escape
Camouflage is their means of survival
While their parents see off any may-be rival.
So as pebbles and stones they will still stay
Until fully fledged when they'll fly away
But next year they'll return to this same landscape
To find a new partner and make their own scrape.

△ 'It was only a lorry, don't be scared'.
Young Plover about to learn the highway code. ▽

My Cabbage Patch Doll

As I have already mentioned in the story on The Farm, most of the occupants nest in all sorts of crops. The Yellow Wagtails are no exception and I don't think there is any crop that they have not nested in. Each year the Wagtails arrive from their wintering grounds in West Africa to nest on the farm so what little help we can give them we do.

My favourite pair nested in a field of cabbages and as usual it was Garry while driving his tractor, who found the nest. Unfortunately the cabbages were ready for picking but with Charles Bransden's permission we were allowed to leave a certain amount of cabbages around the nest.

This is always a risk as we've tried it in the past and it highlights the nest from above. This makes the resident Crows more inquisitive and quite a lot of nests have been raided. But farm cropping has to go ahead so what chance we can give the nesting birds we do.

Some nests I've used the chicken wire method which I place like a cage over the nest and camouflage it. It has not always worked, but when a nest is left exposed it's always worth

△ A few eggs in a few cabbages.
▽ The hen bird visits the nest.

a try and any success is worthwhile. About twenty cabbages were left in the ground around the nest and I erected a hide just a few yards away to help deter the Crows. Both Garry and myself kept a watch out for the brooding bird which hatched five healthy young chicks.

The opportunity to photograph these courageous little birds rearing their family was not to be missed. Many happy hours were spent in the hide photographing or just watching the Wagtails coming to and fro among the cabbages.

Whenever Garry and myself see a successful brood like these we know there is a good chance that the following year our cabbage patch dolls may return once again from their West African winter residence.

▲ Another visit and and another check. Dad keeps a look-out. ▽

▲ Both birds proudly look at their family.

Learning about Lapwings the Hard Way

In my early days of bird photography I attempted to photograph what I thought would be an easy bird, the Lapwing. That was my first mistake, but what a lot I learned about this fascinating bird. The Lapwing is another of our ground nesting birds and there were several pairs in a field adjacent to Kempton Park racecourse.

The usual precautions were made when erecting the hide and everything seemed to be going to plan. That was until my first session with the camera. On entering the field all the nesting Lapwings took to the air. I was soon settled in the hide awaiting their return with interest.

Interest was an understatement as I was about to find out. The nest that I was focussed on must have had the spookiest Lapwing I've ever seen. All the Lapwings soon returned and gradually one by one approached and settled down on their nests. That was all except one (you've guessed it) who for some unknown reason would venture to within six feet of her eggs and settle down on an imaginary nest time and time again. All around me the other birds were happily brooding. Eventually my bird approached her eggs and I was about to press the shutter when all the Lapwings took to the air again. A cyclist had entered the field at the far end but once he had gone all the Lapwings came back and quickly settled down again on their nests.

That was all except one bird (you've guessed again). Once more she went through the same ritual until finally settling down on her eggs. I just watched her until she seemed relaxed before attempting a photograph. I was too late, for up again, all the Lapwings took to the air to see off a pair of Magpies. Then it was the turn of the Crows. Then the Heron who flew over from the nearby Heronry. Not to mention the farmer, several dog walkers, ramblers, more Magpies and Crows, the list was endless. Six hours later and just three photographs, I left my hide of hidden torture.

I learnt more about the Lapwing that day than I could read in any book, and I suppose that could be why I got hooked on bird photography.

Lapwings like most birds have their own territory, but as I mentioned when danger arrives they become as one to see it off. Not to mention seeing off one very new and inexperienced photographer. But I learnt so much that day that I would like to put in print 'thank you Lapwings'.

◁ Eventually the Lapwings returned.

△ My bird settles down at last.　　　　　▽ All the waiting was worthwhile.

The Wet & Dry Skylarks

Another bird that does quite well on The Farm is the Skylark even though it's on the decline in most parts of the country. This pair with just a little help survived the resident Crows, Magpies and the water irrigator.

The Skylarks decided to build their nest in a field of spring onions which did not give them much cover. Garry, while working found the nest and as usual, marked it with a pair of posts. A hide was worked in gradually over a week until it was in a favourable position.

The parent birds were both very cooperative during incubation and after the chicks had hatched out. I took some very rewarding photographs and as Cliff and myself quite often do, I spent a few sessions in the hide just watching and studying the Skylarks' behaviour.

The hide also gave the birds added security as it deters the Crows that are ever present on the farm.

Everything was going fine until one evening I arrived at the farm only to see that the field was being watered by the automatic water irrigator.

There was no time to contact the farmer so I took a chance and made up a shelter over the nest with rocks and a flat piece of stone as a roof.

I sat back and watched one of the parent birds return to the nest, which gave me some hope. After an hour or so the irrigator had passed over the nest and was continuing further up the field.

I approached the nest with caution and a feeling of apprehension, I looked down to see the young chicks laying motionless and cold in a nest of water. My efforts were in vain and I left the scene thinking 'if only I had arrived earlier'. On reaching home, I phoned Garry and told him, he was as upset as I was.

The following morning he went to check the nest on his tractor, but just before he reached it he noticed one of the adult Skylarks with a beak full of feed. He stopped the tractor and watched the bird approach the nest and then fly off with its beak empty. Through his binoculars he could see the other Skylark brooding.

But after the story I had told him he did not hold out much hope, as he could just make out one of the young lying dead beside the sitting bird.

After some ten minutes the other bird returned with more feed and its brooding mate flew off to reveal a movement in the nest. Gary took a closer look to see three young chicks looking quite healthy. Though it is not advisable to interfere with a nest or young, this was an instance where help was needed. I gave that help and my reward was to see the young Skylarks being fed away from the nest which gave me a feeling of contentment.

◀ Danger looms.
First the young had to be kept warm

Dried out chicks now being fed.
Danger over, time to relax.

Dabbling with a Dabchick (or Little Grebe)

One of the main features on The Farm is the pond that Greenhams Construction Materials Ltd created after extracting gravel from the land. It's now quite mature and plays host to several nesting birds, such as Coots, Mallard, Reed Warblers, Whitethroats to name a few.

A pair of Swans have tried for the last two years but unfortunately the resident fox found out and took the eggs. Also a pair of Little Grebes (or Dabchicks) after several skirmishes with the Coots now also use the pond as their Springtime home.

I decided to watch them closer and put a hide up in a nearby reed-bed. What followed was some of the best birdwatching I've seen around the farm. The Grebes had built their nest with rotting vegetation and as always tucked it away beneath a bank-side bush. I watched the eggs being laid, both birds taking their turn in brooding and much more.

They are a fascinating little bird and very secretive. When danger appears they will always dive beneath the surface of the water before emerging some way off.

Four chicks were hatched and all was going well with both birds coming to and fro to feed them in their private little corner of the pond. Then all hell broke loose as a Coot ventured too close. One of the Grebes flew across the water at the Coot and as I thought it was about to crash into it head-first it dived under the water. Then it re-appeared just behind the Coot and gave an alarm call which not only made the Coot jump but also made it mad.

The Coot then flew at the Grebe, but before I could blink the Grebe was gone again. This was confusing me as an onlooker so what it was doing to the Coot, god only knows. But the Little Grebe's ploy had worked, for it had now lured the enemy far away from its young. It then gave one more alarm call before once again disappearing.

By this time the Coot's head must have been spinning, as mine was. While all this had been going on the other Grebe had gathered her young back to the nest and as I watched, her mate returned triumphantly.

Even this I found amusing as he would only show is head above the water. This he did for some time until he was sure that there was no more danger. Then the four chicks got up onto the nest while both parent birds searched for food which they brought back at regular intervals.

This was also interesting as the food supply was varied and included small fish, damsel and dragon flies, other insects plus of all things newts.

I spent many hours watching the Little Grebe family as they kept to this one corner of the pond. I hope they return next year as I would like to see a repeat performance.

◁ 'I'll brood, you feed'.　　　△ 'Is the coast clear'.

▲ Feeding time.
◀ One hatched, three to go.
The Little Grebe sits at ease. ▽

Remember Jim? I shall never forget him. It was Jim who first told me about the Little Ringed Plovers on the gravel pit where he worked. He told me that he had seen a similar bird, but slightly bigger. Of course I went to see it and was delighted to see another new bird in my area, the Ringed Plover. But they seemed to be forever feuding with the smaller Little Ringed Plovers.

Over the following years there became a mutual understanding between the Plovers and now both species nest locally on the gravel pits, but more so on the farm (at Laleham).

One such pair that return each year seem to pick a different crop to nest in, this time it was in a field of fennel. As usual a hide was worked in gradually over a period of time with the permission of Charles Bransden, the farmer. But this time with a lot more caution for in the past I've found the Ringed Plover to be a very nervous bird. This pair of Plovers were obviously used to the farm workers and were to become star material for my book.

Both Garry (tractor driver) and myself checked on the nest over the days to follow. Then one evening I noticed that one egg was

▲ Brooding the eggs.

chipping. When I returned home I phoned my client who I was decorating for and told her I would not be at work the following day as something had cropped up.

She was very understanding because she said 'enjoy your bird watching but tell me all about it the next time I see you'.

I arrived at the hide early the next morning loaded up with sandwiches and a flask of tea. The egg that was chipping revealed a little beak and one of the other eggs had also started to chip. The weather was good and I sat back in the hide with great expectations. I was not disappointed as I watched several change-overs and watched both birds turning the eggs.

I could actually hear the brooding bird talking to the chicks in the eggs which in turn answered back. This I found very fascinating to both watch and hear. But to watch an actual hatch is something very special.

The sitting bird started to get very fidgety and chirping more excitedly before getting up to reveal her first new-born chick. She then picked up the eggshell and ran off some twenty

△ The first born arrives at last.

△ Getting rid of the evidence.　▽ Dad came to have a look.

yards away to dispose of it, just as I had seen the Little Ringed Plovers do.

She was soon back to clean up her first baby before settling down to brood again. This seemed a good time for a cuppa and a round of sandwiches.

After my second cup of tea I was about to leave this family scene when the cock bird called and returned to his sitting mate. Up she got and from beneath her the little chick answered and ran off to his dad.

Dad then brooded it for a short while before getting up to let his first-born pick around the soil for its first meal. At this moment Garry passed close by on his tractor and the hen bird left the nest.

This was my cue to leave also. I went off to work and after telling my client all about my morning, I then proceeded to finish her decorating. On the way home I stopped off at the farm and through my binoculars I could see both birds feeding alongside their, now three chicks. I was happy, my client was happy and I guess so too were the five Ringed Plovers.

Second Ringed Plover

△ This bird did not scare.   This bird did not care. ▽

As I have mentioned the Ringed Plover is usually a very wary bird. so I was very surprised when walking along the beach near Pagham in Sussex, I came across a Ringed Plover that was exactly the opposite. I first noticed it walking away from me somewhat furtively.

I walked on but keeping an eye on the bird and watched it walk back before settling down on the shingle beach. I could see by her behaviour that she had a clutch of eggs. I then walked back towards the sitting bird, but to my astonishment she sat tight.

I was at this time carrying my camera, so I thought that maybe I might get a photograph of some kind to support this short story. This was my next surprise, I finished sitting no more than six feet from her. I took a whole roll of film while she happily brooded and she even stood up and turned the eggs for me. I then slowly stood up and walked away from this remarkable little bird. This was more proof that like us, birds are also very individual at times.

Reed Bunting v Stoats

She watches out for the Stoat.
Emergency over, time to feed.

It was a beautiful Sunday morning as I walked around the local gravel pit. I knew there were two pairs of Reed Buntings nesting at the far side of the pit and I decided to try and locate them. After I had been sitting and watching for a while a cock Reed Bunting made his presence felt by sitting on a tall thistle and giving his brooding mate his alarm call. As I walked on, the female bird flew up not more than five yards from where I had been sitting.

She had a clutch of five eggs in a nest built in the long grass not far from a footpath. I carried on walking and heard the distinctive call of a Kingfisher. I looked over to the far side of the gravel pit and picked out its turquoise blue colour, shining in the morning sun. I watched it feeding for a short time and then moved on again.

Then, just to the left of me there was a rustling in the bank-side vegetation and a pair of Reed Buntings were flittering about frantically. I trained my binoculars to where the noise was coming from and I saw what I thought was a water rat. As I approached and got closer, to my surprise and delight, out from the undergrowth following their parents, were three young Stoats. I stood motionless and watched them walk across my path and into some nearby nettles, the Reed Buntings still in an alarmed state.

A fisherman close by had seen me and came over and asked me what I was looking at. I told him to stand still and look to his right and we both saw three inquisitive little faces peering at us . . . and then they were gone.

The fisherman told me that he had never seen a Stoat before and it had made his morning worthwhile as he hadn't seen a fish either. He went back to his fishing and I watched two relieved Reed Buntings dropping into the undergrowth with their beaks full of grubs.

The Sparrowhawk

My story starts the day I returned home after a few days away.

While taking the last suitcase from the car a Sparrowhawk swooped from nowhere to take a small bird no further than six feet from me. This was the third kill I had seen in the last couple of weeks.

My interest now high, the following week I searched every likely nesting site in my surrounding area, but with no success. Then one evening, while walking around the gravel pit at the back of my house, the hawk attempted another kill. This time the prey was a Mistle Thrush. The bird missed and flew up to land on an old used Crow's nest. On approaching she flew off and I thought this was the end of my long search.

The following days I checked the nest but nothing, once again I had missed out. I continued to walk home watching a few rabbits scuttling to and fro among the nettles and on looking up for no particular reason, I noticed an old Jay's nest. It was now bigger as a crow used it last year.

A tail was visible over the side of it and I at once thought it was a resident Crow. Another look through the binoculars, yes! a Sparrowhawk, I almost let out a shout of glee. I rushed home and rang my friend, Cliff and after explaining the location of the nest he came over with Dave to see if it would be a worthwhile proposition to photograph.

'Brilliant', he said, after scaling some 40 feet up the tree, 'she's got four eggs and we've got to try it'.

I gained permission from RMC Leisure Sports to put up a 'hide' and the following Saturday we were putting up the first few

❖ Mum stands proudly over her brood.

scaffold poles. Two more visits and 40 feet of scaffolding were in place, the rest was left to me.

The hide had to be canvas draped and finally it had to be completed ready for the first stint of photography.

Then it happened, the weather changed to strong winds causing the scaffold to twist and the canvas to blow away. It hung in the tree for the next two days.

On the next Saturday I retrieved the canvas and frame from the lake below the nest. After drying it out Cliff and myself set about re-erecting the hide.

The hide back in position I left Cliff to have the first photographic session. He phoned me later to say everything was worthwhile and I must have a go with the camera the following day. This I did. What was to follow made me also realise all the preparation was worth it.

Loaded up with my camera equipment and a feeling of excitement I set off. At last I reached the bottom of the scaffold, full of anticipation. The hen bird was sitting tight on her clutch of four eggs.

After reaching the top of the scaffold she silently dropped off the nest and glided to a nearby tree. I quickly entered the hide and before I could set up my camera the bird was back at the nest. This bird was to become star material for the next two weeks.

Once at the nest nothing would make her leave, so photography was made easy. During the next week three young were hatched and many rolls of film were developed.

Each of us would spend up to three hours at a time in the hide capturing every possible picture we could. She would sit brooding. Her three chicks resembled tiny cotton wool balls with eyes.

The only time she would leave the nest was when her mate called to her very softly from a nearby tree. She was off and back within thirty seconds with a dead, plucked bird that he had given her.

She would rip the prey to bits offering in turn to each chick the smallest bits of flesh, while she ate the legs or any other rough part.

Then after cleaning up the nest she would bend her talons up and walk across the nest on her knuckles so as not to harm her young. Then, once in position, she would slowly lower herself down onto the chicks and proceed to brood them.

⬧ She brings a ready-plucked bird from her mate.

Many sessions were shared and many moments were captured, like the day she saw a Wood Pidgeon fly into a tree close by, followed by another, and in a split second she was off the nest taking the second bird in mid air.

Then there was the fox that would often pass under the scaffold mid afternoons. Too many incidents to write down, but most captured by the ever clicking cameras.

During the two weeks we were allowed to have the hide up, the weather became very changeable and the scaffold moved some two feet at the top!

But it was all worthwhile and after dismantling out hide there was an air of mixed sadness and happiness. A once in a lifetime experience gone, but three new lives were safe and sound.

I still visited the nest every day watching the chicks getting bigger, until the parent birds stopped feeding them and just dropped the dead prey for themselves to sort out. I watched many a tug-of-war carried out at the nest.

The young Sparrowhawks were now reasonably safe as quite often when I checked them out I would be dive bombed by one of the adult hawks.

But there was to be one more hurdle ahead. The storms arrived and the heavens opened up all night long. I got up early the following morning. It was still raining. I went to the nest with fingers crossed and holding my breath.

I should have known better, for there was mum with wings stretched out, sheltering her almost full-grown chicks who were looking down at me somewhat wet and bedraggled but safe!

A few days have now passed and all that's left is an empty nest, a shelf full of photographs and some very special memories of some very special birds.

▲ A caring mother looks on.
A wet mum, but dry young in the rain.▶

SPARROW HAWK

He sits in the tree way out of sight,
His next meal being another birds' plight.
With piercing eyes he looks around,
For any small bird that may be found.
He'll single one out to persue a kill,
Then swooping down with uncanny skill.
His talons clutch one small lonely bird,
It's cries of pain are seldom heard.
Feathers fly and a life is lost,
But food must be caught at any cost

Kestrels' Unkindly Cut

I'm not about to preach but when I read that the motorways attract Kestrels I just wish the people who say this would realise that the Kestrels were already there before the motorways cut through their habitat. Which leads me to some other kind of cutting.

A local tree surgeon cut down an old tree not realising that it held a nest of six Kestrels. I had a phone call from Jim a Budgerigar breeder (not Jim of the gravel pits) who told me he had been handed a cardboard box containing the young Kestrels and he asked me what he should do with them.

At that time I was not too sure, so Jim attempted to hand rear them with a little help from someone more of an expert than me.

Jim kept the young birds indoors, where each bird claimed its own part of the house. One decided that the telephone would make a nice perch. From then on each incoming phone call became a risk to answer it.

Six Kestrels meant a regular supply of dead chicks. Six Kestrels meant six lots of bird droppings. You can imagine the state of the house while Jim was rearing them. Jim had a very understanding wife.

The end result for Jim's endeavours was six healthy full grown Kestrels that were eventually released back into the wild in the correct procedure.

⬆ The Kestrel at its nest hole.

A few years have since passed and Jim no longer breeds Budgies, but is now into wine making in a big way. Perhaps all the trials and tribulations with the Kestrels made him turn to drink.

⬇ Jim proudly displays one of the young.

THE KESTREL

He hovers above with head so still
Surveying the ground to make a kill
His flapping wings seem to be a blur
As he looks below for his prey to stir
A bird, a mouse or even a vole
He's not fussy what fills a hole
For back at the nest his chicks are greedy
And without any food become more needy
So his hunting technique goes on all day
Until at last he catches his prey.

Working for Woodpeckers

△ The Woodpeckers lofty hide.
◁ The male Lesser Spotted Woodpecker.
The female Lesser Spotted Woodpecker. ▽

As I mentioned in my introduction both Cliff and I have our own favourite birdwatching areas. One of his is a little patch close to his home in Abinger, where all three species of Woodpeckers breed.

It's a nice quiet secluded area with lots of old mature trees and has a small stream that meanders through it. Badgers have a set on the edge of the wooded area.

It's a place where you can sit and watch nature as it should be, undisturbed and peaceful. We have watched and photographed all three species of Woodpeckers, but the Lesser Spotted gave us the hardest time of the three.

Being one of Cliff's favourite areas he worked hard to locate this little bird. After many hours of patient watching he found a nesting hole high up in a silver birch that was barely visible from the ground. In fact, I could hardly detect it through my binoculars.

Cliff then erected a hide and seeing that the nest hole was some fifty feet from the ground, it was no mean feat. But once again it was well worth the effort as some of the photographs he took were excellent.

▲ The Green Woodpecker.
The Great Spotted Woodpecker. ▲

Cliff has the occasional picture published in the magazine 'Birdwatching' and the Lesser Spotted Woodpecker is one of them. I had just one session in the hide that turned out to be somewhat of a disaster. When photographing, some days you just can't get the right feel of the situation. It's very hard to explain, sometimes it is down to concentration.

This day seemed to be one that I could not get my brain into gear. So the day my slides dropped through the letter box I quickly placed the litter bin next to me before opening them. Although the couple of hours I spent in the hide was brilliant birdwatching I did not hold out much hope of getting a decent photograph.

I was dejectedly flicking my box of thirty six slides into the litter bin when bingo! there were the two slides I wanted.

All of a sudden those two hours spent in the hide was relived and the two slides were my bonus, thanks to Cliff.

The Abinger (Yellow) Hammer

Since moving to Shepperton, what Yellow Hammers there were have now disappeared. Over in Cliff's area of Abinger there are still a few pairs about. So when Cliff phoned me about a pair that were nesting on a local plantation I was obviously keen to go and watch them.

He had already moved a hide into a good position. We drove up in Cliff's open back truck to watch the birds flying to their nest with feed. Then from nowhere the cock bird was attacked by a Sparrowhawk. They both dropped to the ground close to the nest, in a flash Cliff leapt from the cab and ran over towards the birds.

The Hawk flew up and landed on top of the hide for a split second before disappearing out of sight. I followed over and we both looked down at the nest with relief as the Yellow Hammer had escaped the talons of the Sparrow Hawk. But it was obviously in a state of shock as it sat still for quite some while before it stood upright, checked on its young prior to walking off very gingerly into the undergrowth before flying off.

A few days later I spent two pleasant hours in the hide watching the Yellow Hammers. Whilst in the hide I had what we call a bonus visit.

I could hear a noise that I had not heard before and it was getting closer to the hide. I looked out to see the foliage moving about just behind the hide. Then the head of a Red Legged Partridge appeared. This was the first one I had ever seen in the wild and it was a female.

Just to the left of me the undergrowth was moving and out of it came a cock bird calling to the hen. Time for one quick photo and then they were gone and not long after so was I.

I was off to a second location of Cliff's, his local stream and its star attraction the Kingfisher. Later that week Cliff had been in the Yellow Hammer's hide and had the Sparrowhawk chasing the bird to the nest again.

Once more Cliff saw it off and we both hoped that the family survived this persistent hunter. But this is what makes nature sometimes cruel, but always interesting.

◀ The cock bird visits.   ⬠ The hen bird visits.   ▽ A Red Legged Partridge visits.

A Deer Interlude

I live not far from Bushy Park where I can watch both Fallow and Red Deer at my leisure. The best time for me is the rutting season which at times can be very exciting.

I always carry my camera when I'm in the park and by doing so I've been lucky enough to capture some pleasing photographs. Like the time a Fallow Deer was standing in the early morning mist, as I thought to myself 'if only the sun would break through'. Sure enough it did and I was able to get the picture I wanted.

Then there was the day while walking my dog 'Freda' I noticed a female deer acting strangely before running off some hundred yards and stopping to look back. I ventured over to the spot that she had left to find a new born fawn with the afterbirth still by its side. I took two photographs before quickly retiring well away to watch her return to tend to her new baby.

Another day, well into the rutting season I came across an old Stag that was resting up in the bracken. He had been over indulging in the true spirit of the rut or was just plum tuckered out anyway he did not seem to mind one happy photographer.

◁ The sun broke through at last.   △ Where's my mother'?
▽ Not much cover.   He's overbred or overfed. ▷

A Close-up on Grebes

Because it's one of our early-nesting birds I guess I've studied the Great Crested Grebe more than any other bird.

In the first weeks of February I've listened and watched as these beautiful water birds put on their courtship display. Many times I've heard them on the gravel pit at the back of our house calling out all night long. I have so many memories of encounters with these birds that I could write a book on Grebes alone. But here is just one.

This particular pair nest every year on a little backwater of the River Thames at Lower Sunbury. With the rise and fall of the river they are forever repairing their nest, which they always build on the branches of a tree which lies in the water. I've spent many hours watching and photographing them as no hide was needed.

I paid the Grebes a visit as I knew they should be hatching out at any time, but when I arrived I found both birds acting in an agitated manner, and I could also detect a young chick in the feathers of the Grebe that was sitting on the nest.

I had missed the hatching of the chicks but I was more concerned about the adult birds behaviour. Then a man appeared on the far bank who I had met on a previous visit who told me of a Pike that had taken two of the young. He allowed me on to the bank (which was private property) to see for myself and, sure enough, there just below the nest lay a Pike of some 10 pounds.

One of the Grebes was sitting tight with just two of the young left out of the original brood of four. I found a large stick and tried to prod the Pike but I missed. It was enough to scare it off, however, and it disappeared.

When the Grebes felt it was safe they left the nest with their two remaining chicks on mums' back and swam off down stream and out of danger. Once again, with a little luck and a little human assistance two young lives were saved.

As I watched them swim off into the main river, I felt pleased.

THE GREBE

A walk by the lake and maybe a chance,
To watch the Grebes beginning their dance.
A shake of the head while side by side,
Together across the water they glide.
Heads held aloft and beaks full of weed,
A ritual dance seems to be their main need.
Love making all done and four eggs are laid,
On a platform of weed that both birds have made.
Four young are hatched and are ready to feed,
So both birds go fishing to fulfil their need.
'I've caught a fish' one of the Grebes calls,
And towards him swims, four grey feathered balls.
Beaks wide open with only one wish,
But only one baby will swallow the fish.
This scene I shall watch for many a day,
Until the young have grown up and then fly away.
This bird of beauty that was once nearly dead,
For their feathers once adorned many a lady's head.
But now the Grebes are winning for all to see,
Swimming and dancing and fishing and FREE!

◀ The Pike still loomed below.
The changing of the guard. ▲
'Peek-a-boo, I can see you'. ▶
Some weeks later and time for a nap. ▼

Persevering Swans

The Swans returned to their annual nesting site, a small island on the River Thames at Shepperton, to be met by a pair of angry Geese that had taken up residence. After several skirmishes they gave up and proceeded to build a nest a few yards away from the island in the middle of a sidestream. They had six eggs and were happily going through their parenteral duties of preparing to rear another family, when it happened. There was a terrific downpour of rain that lasted for a few days, causing the river to rise dramatically. The Swans worked furiously to save their nest and clutch of eggs but seemed to be losing the battle, as they could not re-build faster than the rising water.

A few onlookers and myself gathered bundles of wood, branches and twigs and threw them into the water for the cob to pass to his brooding mate to keep the nest and eggs above the water level.

This procedure went on for a couple of weeks with both birds working furiously, twenty four hours a day, non-stop.

All seemed lost as the nest was now nearly four feet high, with the river not receding fast enough. Then one evening I went to check on

⌂ The river was still rising.

the birds, the level of the water had dropped and there was a movement under the sitting swan. She was looking proud and her mate, although rather shattered, was sitting along-side watching on with interest. After watching for a short while, one little grey head appeared from beneath its mother, who promptly gave it a loving peck before it disappeared again.

I returned the following morning to find a nest two feet above the water with no signs of the swan family.

I returned home and walked down to the edge of the gravel pit that backs onto my garden and to my surprise there, on the bank, were the pair of swans standing proudly with six fluffy cygnets. This was truly amazing as I live about one mile from their nest.

After a few minutes the parents seemed to give a triumphant call and swam off with their family, leaving me with an equally great feeling of satisfaction. This was nature at its most rewarding best.

◁ The Swans work furiously to save their nest and eggs.

THE SWAN

The graceful Swan is a sight to see
On Pond or Lake or Estuary
The Cob stakes his claim on one of these
To court his mate with amorous pleas
With necks entwined they show their emotion
These swans who share a life of devotion.

◀ The Geese take their family for a drink at the local.
With this sight, I breathed a sigh of relief. ▲
Bottoms up! the hard work was worth it. ▼

The Rule-Breaking Mistle Thrushes

◁ 'A few worms needed here'.

W hen I hear the Mistle Thrush in full song way up high in the top of a tree I know another breeding season is not too far away.

Being one of our early breeders it is often heard singing on a windy day as early as January. Sometimes it's nest is built in an exposed position as most trees are not in full leaf. This makes the birds very wary and sometimes very aggressive to anybody or anything that gets too close to their nest. So I was very surprised when I found a nest just four feet from the ground in the fork of a tree. The Thrushes alarm call at first drew my attention.

Two young Mistle Thrushes at the base of the tree was the reason. Usually I would leave well alone, but there at eye level was the nest with two other young. I picked up the two from off the ground and placed them back in the safety of the nest and then watched from a safe distance.

It soon became clear that these young Thrushes were to say at the least, over active. Every visit to the nest by either parent bird was met by four youngsters that almost catapulted out of the nest. Because the young thrushes were at an advanced stage I could not risk putting up a hide for a possible photo. But they were so photogenic I tried for a couple of pictures.

I set up the camera on a tripod in a nearby bush and attached a cable release. I then sat back well hidden in another bush and waited for the returning birds.

To my delight both birds soon returned with beaks full of feed and seemed to be unaware of my presence. I only took six photographs and when the bird flew off to get more food for their young acrobats I hurriedly left.

A few days later as I always do, I returned to see the parent birds feeding their full family of four away from the nest. This proved that although the Mistle Thrush is a very wary bird, there is always an exception to the rule.

◁ 'One at a time please'.

The Gardener's Friend

THE SONG THRUSH

With speckled chest that's puffed out proud
He sings on high so strong and loud
Each Spring he returns to his favourite tree
To sing for his mate, or is it for me?
For who ever it is I don't really care
Because his is a song I'll willingly share
He'll sing all day for there is no rush
For this beautiful song from our bird the Thrush
The eater of snails and the odd other pest
The gardener's friend with his speckled chest.

Moorhens' Hideaway

I've found Moorhens nesting in all sorts of locations, reeds, bushes, boats and trees (one nest containing 26 eggs, yet another story), but my favourite is the one I shall now describe.

On the gravel pit at the back of my house there have been three barges moored up for about five years. Alongside the barges are a few suspended lorry tyres which Coots, Moorhens and, of all birds, a Tufted Duck, have used for nesting in from time to time. This particular day, I was rowing around the pit ever watchful of any wildlife that might be about, when I saw a bird fly into one of the barges. I was not sure what the bird was so, of course, I investigated.

The sight that met my eyes when I peered over and into the middle barge was remarkable.

◀ Draped in rape.   Tufted Duck, an outside tenant. ▲
A Coot nests close by. ▼

Over the years, water had collected along with seeds carried by the winds or other means to create a wildlife habitat full of wild flowers and grasses.

At one end of the barge was an old tool shed which I entered and waited for the bird I had seen earlier, to make an appearance. I stood there for sometime watching dragon flies and other insects flying to and fro, including a pair of Goldfinches that came to gather seed.

I was about to leave when I heard a Moorhen call and then show itself as it swam out of some rape that had grown in the barge. It carried on swimming towards me unaware of my presence and after climbing onto a nest, which I had not noticed, settled down after turning its eggs. After some minutes had passed the sitting bird started to weave an overhead canopy with the rape flowers. I stood fascinated for the next hour until something stirred the Moorhen, which quickly slid off the nest and disappeared into the surrounding foliage.

I at once left this beautiful setting to return the following day with my camera to capture some remarkable photographs.

Before leaving, I placed a plank of wood up to the edge of the barge so that the young Moorhens had another means of escape from any unforeseen dangers.

This they used as I was fortunate enough to see two of the young dropping off the barge into the water and the safety of the parent birds.

A Little Time with Little Owls

The Owls were nesting in a hole in an old oak tree some twelve feet up. The tree was in a private garden just outside Abinger and the owners had given permission to carry out our photography.

My chance came on a hot Sunday morning and on arriving, Dave a friend of Cliff's was just getting down from the hide. He told me that in two hours he had not seen an owl of any shape or size. The reason being the owners of the garden had been active all morning along with their little Jack Russell dog.

After being introduced to the owners, Dave left for home and breakfast and wished me better luck. Entering the hide with little confidence I set up my camera and tripod. Below I could see the owners pottering about in the garden with the little Jack Russell running to and fro, playing and barking. I sat there thinking I had wasted a journey but what was to follow soon changed my mind.

After about ten minutes the owners and dog retired back inside the cottage, peace at last I thought and sure enough a little grey fluffy head popped up from the hole in the tree followed by another. I watched them for some time before taking a few photographs then out of another hole just below appeared another head, not a fluffy one but the head of the Jack Russell. He had got out of the house and somehow climbed up the inside of the tree and of course the baby owls shot out of sight before I could blink. The dog soon got fed up, climbed down and ran barking towards the house to be let in.

Peace and quiet again and within minutes both baby owls re-appeared. This time my camera was working overtime as I watched

⊳ First there was one.

both birds exploring the nearby branches. Every now and again one of the parent birds would call to them from close by. This was great to watch and when a third fluffy head appeared it was brilliant. All three seemed to be juggling for the best vantage point and several times I thought one would fall but they never did.

The parent bird called again and flew into the tree behind the nest hole. I watched in anticipation, camera at the ready, but she flew off calling and the baby owls dived into the nest hole and out of sight. The reason was a couple of horse riders and their following labradors passed by below. Once out of sight the baby owls were up and out of the hole calling to their parent. In a flash the parent bird flew back carrying a small vole in its beak and it disappeared straight down into the hole followed by its hungry brood. I waited once more, camera focussed on the hole. She popped

◀ Then there were two.
Then there were three. ▽

Then there was me. ▷

up looking straight at the hide, 'click' I got the
photograph I wanted and in a blur she was off.
Soon all three baby Owls were out again and I
took some more pleasing photographs.

Then I sat back for another half an hour or
so savouring every moment while I took a well-
earned drink.

I then packed up my tripod and camera and
on leaving the hide the door of the cottage
opened and our ran the little Jack Russell.
Perfect timing I thought!

Reed Warbler and Cuckoo

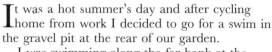

It was a hot summer's day and after cycling home from work I decided to go for a swim in the gravel pit at the rear of our garden.

I was swimming along the far bank at the same time watching the Reed Warblers darting in and out of the waterside reeds collecting food for their young. I noticed one of the nests was leaning over at a very acute angle and after a closer inspection I found the cause, a rather active young Cuckoo.

After securing the nest the best I could, I left the foster parents to complete their exhausting day trying to satisfy this large ball of grey and black feathers.

I returned several days later, the nest had been vacated but the Reed Warblers seemed to be collecting food in a rather frantic fashion. Searching about the reeds I found the young Cuckoo sitting on a submerged branch in the water, its feathers becoming more waterlogged with every movement.

I had to act quickly and after looking around, found an old gate post which I managed to stick in the bank.

I then, with some difficulty, got hold of the now soaking wet Cuckoo and placed it on the gate post. All the time the Reed Warblers were flitting about me excitedly. Fortunately the sun was warm and this helped the Cuckoo's feathers to dry out. I then retreated to a safe distance behind some cover to watch the outcome. The Reed Warbler soon flew to the Cuckoo and after checking that it was ok proceeded to collect food for it.

I sat fascinated watching these two small birds feed this young dustbin at an incredible rate, sometimes actually perching on its back to feed it.

After about an hour the Cockoo's feathers had dried out in the afternoon sunshine. This caused the bird to try several attempts to fly to safety but each time it fluttered to the ground and each time I replaced it on the post. Eventually it managed to flutter up to a branch of a nearby

◀ 'How do I feed it'?

overhanging willow tree. The Warblers now seemed more at ease and continued to fill the Cuckoo's large red mouth with all sorts of waterside insects and grubs.

I left this unforgettable scene savouring every moment and knowing I had once again helped nature to succeed.

The Cuckoo was reared successfully as I often saw it whilst walking around the gravel pit, still of course being fed by its overworked foster parents.

THE REED BED FILLED WITH FEAR

The Warblers return to the reed bed
happy to build their new nest
but there's a sound that they all dread
it's the sound of an unwanted guest.
The reed bed becomes a silent place
as the Warblers try their best
to hide and make them hard to trace
from this large intruding pest.
For the Cuckoo's back again this year
to deposit her eggs – one per nest
filling the reeds with annual fear
and giving the Warblers much unrest.
Once the Cuckoos' young's hatched out
food must be gathered come what may
it must be fed for there's no doubt
it gets much bigger every day.
These foster parents have a task
to fill the young one's needs
and to give it everything it asks
while it sits there in the reeds.
But in this world of nature
this scene is nothing new
for this happens every year
to raise just one Cuckoo.
And when it's fledged it flies away
only to return another year
to lay it's eggs sometime in May
in the reed bed filled with fear.

◀ Where there's a will there's a way.
No cuckoo means one relaxed warbler. ▽

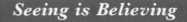

The Aptly-Named Wagtails

◀ 'Please don't start up the engine'.
▼ Pied Wagtails in the cress beds.

The two other British Wagtails are resident birds and both nest in another of Cliff's birdwatching haunts, on the watercress beds not far from his home. He has permission to birdwatch and photograph on the land.

Both birds have nested in an old workshop close by. The Pied Wagtail chose the upstairs one year and the Grey Wagtail, downstairs among some old machinery and piles of wood.

On both occasions Cliff, as always, had a hide in place which resulted in some very rewarding watching and some excellent photography.

The Grey Wagtail is usually found nesting not too far from water and at one of Cliff's favourite sites one had nested in a roll of barbed wire hanging on a wall. Where as the Pied Wagtail nests almost anywhere, cranes, flower pots, car engines, an old bread bin to name a few.

But the most daring pair I knew of, nested under the seat of Garry's tractor on The Farm. Not only did the Wagtails take turns in brooding the eggs while Garry was driving the tractor, they actually reared their young by following the tractor up and down the field and when it stopped flew in and under the seat, then off again to gather more feed. For obvious reasons it was impossible to capture a photograph of this cheeky pair.

◀ This Wagtail bred in a breadbin.

△ A barbed wire fortress.

▽ Grey Wagtails in the cress beds.

A Tern's Turn

⌂ 'When I'm calling you'.

My friend Ron had telephoned me about a pair of Terns that had nested in the local water works filter beds.

We visited the site to find that they had actually nested on the walkway between the beds. Looking at the sitting bird from a distance we wondered how we could possibly get a photograph without disturbing her.

With a lot of thought we agreed it wasn't on and began to walk back to the car. A workman in a small tipper truck was driving along in front of us and started to turn down towards the sitting Tern. We managed to stop him only for him to tell us that he knew about the bird and had been driving past her for days. This he did once more which did not seem to bother the Tern.

Ron and I both realised that if the tipper driver could do it then so could we. After gaining permission to drive our cars along the same route as the workman, we positioned our cameras inside and started off slowly towards the Tern.

Ron stopped the car within a few yards from the Tern and waited to see what would happen. She sat tight and it was obvious to us that she had young beneath her as her feathers were all fluffed out.

Sure enough, within a few minutes a little face appeared from under her mother's wing, followed by another.

We sat motionless as the parent bird looked skywards and called to her mate who landed nearby with a small fish in his beak. As he approached her she got up and three chicks raced towards their dad, the winner getting the prize. Then he settled down with the young and she flew off, obviously to feed and return later with food for the chicks.

We had not taken one photograph whilst this was all happening, but all was not lost because after a patient wait she returned with another fish. Our cameras clicked away from inside the car capturing many fine family portraits.

This was birdwatching and photography in comfort as it started to drizzle with rain. After a short time we drove off slowly leaving the three little balls of fluff dry and secure beneath their now wet mother, or was it dad?

▽ A view from a car.

Outfoxed Terns

A pair of Terns that return each year to the raft that Bill and Richard built. Over the years the silt on the gravel pit has built up around the raft so I thought it was time to photograph the Terns for the record.

That was easier said than done as it mean't laying several scaffold boards and a pallet on top of six feet of boggy silt. But I did eventually manage it and erected a hide on top of the pallet (I don't advise anyone to try to copy me).

Each time I arrived at the gravel pit one of the Terns would dive bomb me with its beak clicking away until I was out of sight.

The Terns accepted the hide and many rewarding photographs were taken. Two chicks hatched out and after a day's work I would pop along to the hide just to watch them. On arriving one evening I could see that one of the chicks had fallen from the raft and was now vulnerable to the Crows, Magpies and Herons that were always on the look-out for an easy meal. I felt helpless as there was no way I could reach it over the silt. But after watching a

▵ I trod carefully.   One good Tern deserves another. ▵ ▵
One good Tern deserves a mother. ▵

Heron being seen off by the Terns I felt more at ease.

I then realised that the chick would have to be fed, so I sat back in the hide and patiently waited in the hope that I might just get a photograph of it happening.

The young Tern was some way away when one of the adult birds arrived back with a small fish. I managed just one photograph before leaving for home.

I returned the following day to see that although the Terns had seen off the Crows, Magpies and Herons they had been helpless with a Fox.

All I could see was its footprints to and from a now empty raft. But to end this little story on a happier note, the following year water was pumped onto the silt and the raft became Fox-free. Hence two triumphant Terns once more.

Dippers' Delight

Cliff has for many years spent at least one week a year away, to photograph birds, and some of his experiences no doubt will be published in his own book.

I have joined him for the last three years, firstly to Wales, then France and Wales again. We gathered enough stories to write a second book but I've got to sell this one first, so here is just two of them.

On one of our trips to Wales our main aim was to photograph a Dipper, and after checking out what seemed to be every bridge on the local river we eventually found one pair nesting under an overhanging bank not far from where we were staying.

We set up a heavy metal framed hide in the shallows and weighted it down with large rocks. The next day I had the first session in the hide.

Tripods and flash guns were set up in the river just in front of the hide. Everything was checked before Cliff left me to it for an agreed hour, and what an hour it turned out to be.

This was to be my first close-up of a pair of Dippers. The first bird to return was the cock bird, who flew low towards me from upstream. He landed on a nearby rock as I waited with camera focussed on the nest. But he seemed intent on singing his head off.

I looked out of one side flap and then the other, but I could see no dipper. Then I looked out of the front of the hide only to see him perched up on one of the flash guns. After several flicks of his tail he flew up to the nest to feed his young before flying back to the flash guns whereon he burst into song again.

His mate then appeared from downstream before carrying out the same procedure less the singing. I sat in the hide for the full hour in awe of these little birds and their antics.

When Cliff arrived I told him that I had not taken one photograph, but what I had witnessed had been breathtaking. After his turn in the hide he came out with exactly the same feeling.

◀ A Dipper carrying feed.
The rippling waters that gather at speed. ◭

Many hours were spent watching the Dippers even after the skies had opened up one night and the river rose to within inches of their nest.

Less important was our hide, hanging in a bankside bush some way downstream. Once the water had stopped running off the surrounding hills the river level dropped enough for the Dippers to survive.

In the days to follow I watched both birds lead a pair of Jays away from their nest by using the same diversions as I had seen the Little Grebes do to the Coots back home on The Farm lake. By showing themselves close to the Jays before disappearing below the water and re-appearing further downstream.

Then there was the Heron which came stalking along the river looking for an easy meal. Luckily I was in the hide and a quick wave of my hand through the side flap made sure it would not be back. Cliff had a Buzzard perch on a branch overhanging the river not far from the Dippers' nest.

These scenes were all added bonuses and every evening after a full day's birdwatching and photography we always got around to discussing our brave little water birds. They will always have a special place in my memories.

THE DIPPER

This brave little bird that takes no heed
Of the rippling waters that travel at speed
Is the bold bird the Dipper who's looking his best
In chocolate brown with his little white vest
With a flick of his tail and a bob of his head
He disappears to search the river bed
For Caddis Grubs and little fishes
To satisfy his young ones wishes.

Redstarts in the Rain

The evening before we were leaving Wales I found a Redstart nesting in an old wall of a nearby woodshed. Although I had found other Redstart nests during the week, the cock bird always seemed to be very wary. This one was the opposite, in fact he was very bold.

On showing Cliff my find we both agreed he was worth photographing. We had to work quickly for we had very little time, so we set up a hide on top of some bales of hay before returning back to our base for a cup of tea and another talk about the Dippers. We were up early the next morning, but so was the rain.

Cliff saw me into the hide before returning to pack his bags and load up the van. He had no sooner gone when there as bold as brass was the cock Redstart perched up on a post with a beak full of feed. Just behind him but nowhere near as bold was his mate.

After a short while he flew up to the side of the wall and perched up on what looked like an old metal spike. I did not take a photograph for fear of spoiling what could possibly be star material for the rest of my session in the hide. He then flew into a crack in the wall to feed his young before returning to show himself back on the spike.

The time seemed right, so I took a photograph, then another and before I knew it I had taken half a roll of film before he flew

◀ The bold cock Redstart.

off. I then waited for the female Redstart to perch up on the spike, but no such luck, as she was in, fed her young and out again before I could blink.

Soon her mate was back to do a bit more posing and in no time at all, I took the second half of the film. I quickly reloaded the camera and waited once more as it would not be long before Cliff would be returning.

'May be I might just get one photograph of the female' – I was thinking – when I could hear the sound of our van coming up the track. I looked through the lens and there she was, perched on the spike. I managed just two shots before Cliff pulled-up to take his turn in the hide.

It was now raining heavier, but as it was Cliff's last chance he gave it a go. I returned in about an hour, with the van loaded up and ready to hit the road home.

Cliff said that although the light was bad he had managed to capture some good material considering the weather.

Within ten minutes the hide was on the van and we were on our way. I took one last look back to see the cock Redstart perched up for another photographic session.

As we reached the motorway we were still talking about the week and the different birds we had seen. The time spent in the Buzzard hide (that's another story) and how the cock Redstart had been so different to the others.

There was then a lull in the conversation before we both said at the same time 'Yes, but what about those Dippers?'.

The bashful female Redstart. ▷

Memories

◁ Picturesque Pied Flycatcher.
Reed Warblers residence. △
A colourful cock Bullfinch. ▷
A settled Sandpiper. ▽
Buzzards in the tree tops. ◁
The Elegant Avocet. ▽ ▽

"Where's my mum?".
"I'm over here" with your Brothers and Sisters.
This Family of Coots delayed the boat owners
trip up the river.
A Female Monagu's Harrier stands guard at her nest.

Common Tern surveys the water below. ▷

▲ Reflections..

▽ A Cock Blackbird feeds his young.

◁ A Swallow feeding it's young (Luckily I was carrying my camera).

▲ A Song Thrush in colourful Winter surroundings.

A bonus shot for Cliff at his Kingfisher Hide. ▷

The Resilient and Brilliant Kingfisher

⚬   The Kingfisher's favourite perch.

I was still thinking about the Yellow Hammers as I arrived at Cliff's other hide on his pair of Kingfishers. I spent another two hours watching both birds bringing small fish back to feed their young up in the safety of their bankside tunnel.

The young were quite big as there was a continual whirring noise from within, and the nest hole was getting messy. This was good for me, as every now and then either adult bird would drop out of the tunnel and into the stream below. Then fly up to a post in the water and preen their feathers before flying off downstream to catch more fishes.

This all made fantastic and relaxing birdwatching. I would have liked to write a story about the Kingfisher because it is a bird that has a continuous struggle to survive. But

⚬   After a quick dip.

what I have got are a some facts about our most colourful British bird.

As I write it is 12th January 1997 and all the local lakes, gravel pits and even the river Thames is frozen across in parts. This is when the Kingfishers numbers decrease for they must have open water to catch their food.

Add to this, pollution, boat traffic and other water sports, they certainly are up against it. But somehow they seem to pull through and one of the reasons I think is that a successful pair can raise up to three broods in a year.

⌂ The Kingfisher's other perch.　⌂ In the mid-day sun.

When I give talks, the majority of audiences will tell me that they have never seen a Kingfisher.

I have studied this courageous little bird over the years and found out so much about them. Cliff's pair for instance, nested in the only bit of bank on a very small brook.

Quite a lot of people locally are anti-gravel, but the Kingfisher has made the gravel pits very much their home. So much so that in my small village of Shepperton there were at least six pairs nesting this year.

Let us assume they all at least double brooded just four young each time, that's at least forty-eight young Kingfishers. As most bird watchers know it is a very secretive bird, but that's a lot of Kingfishers in one small area.

As I said, extremely cold weather definitely reduces their number, so I can only say the Kingfishers of Shepperton are resilient and brilliant birds.

THE KINGFISHER

A patient bird, a regal bird,
A bird that's rarely seen or heard.
A little bird of great esteem,
Some say the jewel of the stream.
His speed on wing is seldom seen,
A flash of blue or is it green?
A shaft of light may pick him out,
As below he watches a tempting trout.
A bob of his head and a furtive glance,
An aim, a dive, he'll take his chance.
A splash, a miss, but he'll try again,
For there's young mouths to feed
on his domain.

▽ Seeing is believing.

Some very sleepy Goslings bring my book to a close

Acknowledgements

I would like to thank just a few people who in some way or another helped me to put my book together.

Ron Wells for introducing me to bird photography.

Bill Lowe for our early learning days in bird photography.

Cliff Reddick a good friend for trying to put me right on bird photography.

Old Jim for all his stories and yarns, be them false or true.

Greenham Construction Materials Ltd for the use of their land, the pond on the farm they helped to create, plus the sponsorship to aid my hobby.

'Freda' my dog, I would just like to mention.

'Sammy' another dog I would like to mention.

All the people who helped to give me the confidence to attempt a book.

Mac of FPS, responsible for the text setting.

Finally, Nick Payne, who I tried to help in his football career, has now helped to finance something I've always wanted, my book, 'Seeing is Believing'